THE
JOKIEST
JOKING CHRISTMAS JOKE BOOK
EVER WRITTEN . . . NO JOKE!

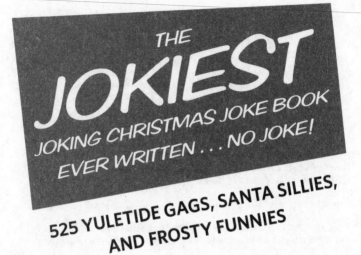

THE JOKIEST JOKING CHRISTMAS JOKE BOOK EVER WRITTEN ... NO JOKE!

525 YULETIDE GAGS, SANTA SILLIES, AND FROSTY FUNNIES

JOKES BY **BRIAN BOONE**

ILLUSTRATIONS BY **AMANDA BRACK**

CASTLE POINT BOOKS
NEW YORK

I just won a
prize for
"Best Snowman."
It was outstanding
in its field.

CONTENTS

INTRODUCING . . .

On chuckles, on laughter, on smiles, on jest! It's a big book of Christmas jokes, isn't that just the best?

Maybe, but the *truly best thing* is the holidays, the most wonderful time of the year! We tend to agree, what with all the excitement, hustle and bustle, decorations, songs, togetherness, giving, receiving, treats, stories, movies, and traditions associated with Christmas. It's all full of joy and seasonal good tidings, and every wonderful part of this holly-jolly thing is celebrated in *The Jokiest Joking Christmas Joke Book Ever...No Joke! 525 Yuletide Giggles, Santa Sillies, and Frosty Funnies.*

Christmas is such a big part of life for so many people, that we thought we'd gift you the best jokes we've ever heard about everything to do with it, straight from Santa's workshop at the North Pole, delivered by reindeer-pulled sleigh to you, right under a tree or inside of a stocking.

So happy ha-ha-holidays, because 'tis the season to be laughing, fa la la la la, la ha ha ha!

1
Ho Ho Ho, Ha Ha Ha
Santa is coming to laugh!

Who keeps
watch over the
North Pole
while Santa is out
delivering toys?
The North Police.

Why does Santa deliver presents?
Because the presents won't deliver themselves.

What does Santa wear on Christmas?
Santa Clothes!

Where does Santa store his red suit?
In the Claus-et.

Why was Santa sick by New Year's Eve?
He kept running into the flue on Christmas.

How much does it cost for Santa to park his sleigh?
Eight bucks.

How can you know that Santa Claus is nearby?
You can sense his presents.

Did you hear that Santa got lost on Christmas Eve?
He was mis-sled.

What happens when Santa goes down a chimney where there's a fire burning?
You get Crisp Cringle.

How much did Santa's sleigh cost?
Nothing—it was on the house!

How can you tell that Santa is great at Taekwondo? He's got a black belt.

What's the best way to
track down Santa Claus?
Follow the Santa clues!

**How did busy Santa find time to fill the
stockings with orange juice?**
He just squeezed it in.

How does Santa make a sleeping bag?
He softly sings "Silent Night" to his bag of toys.

Who brings presents to
the good little sharks?
Santa Jaws.

Did you hear Santa found a house with a security system?
He was alarmed!

Does Santa just head into a fireplace?
No, he makes sure to ash first.

Why is Santa's beard white?
So he can hide out at the North Pole.

Santa was supposed to go to the mall to meet with a bunch of kids, but he couldn't find the right place.
Talk about a lost Claus.

Why are Santa's gardens in such good shape? Because he likes to hoe, hoe, hoe.

What do you call Santa on a break?
Santa Pause.

**Did you hear that somebody tried
to blackmail Santa?**
They sent him their Christmas letter covered in soot.

How does Santa
get in shape
for Christmas?
He works out at
the chimn-asium.

What kind of motorcycle does Santa drive?
A Holly Davidson.

**Why does Santa leave the North Pole
only once a year?**
So he doesn't get ho-ho-homesick.

What's Santa's favorite basketball team?
The St. Knicks.

What happens when you cross Santa
with a horse?
A Santaur.

**What do you call Santa when he bunches
up his nose?**
Kris Crinkle.

What's red and green and rides a sleigh?
Airsick Santa.

Does the ocean greet Santa when he passes over?
Sure, it waves!

What's red, white, red, white, red, white . . . ?
Santa rolling down a hill.

Santa used to be a champion race car driver.
He always seemed to be in the Pole position.

What's gigantic, gray, delivers presents,
and smells like peanuts?
Elephanta Claus.

What does Santa say as he goes back up the chimney?

"Oh, oh, oh!"

How do you clean a sleigh?

With Santa-tizer.

Santa got his outfit dirty in a clogged chimney.

But hey—it soots him!

There's always room in Santa's sleigh for all the toys because he carefully measures things. He measures in Santa-meters.

Who stole Santa's bag of gifts
without being seen?
The Ghost of Christmas Present.

In which state was Santa born?
Ida-ho-ho-ho.

**What's red and white and slowly moves
up and down?**
Santa in an elevator.

Where does Santa spend his summers?
In Santa Fe.

What's red and white and falls down chimneys?
Santa Klutz.

Santa builds houses at the North Pole for all his helpers. But how?
Igloos them.

Who keeps an eye on Santa's workshop?
The sleigh-borhood watch.

What item is Santa always wearing?
A watch!

Are Santa's toys store-bought?
No, they're ho-ho-homemade.

What does Santa knock off his boots when he gets back to the North Pole?
Santa Clods.

Did you know about the layers that keep the North Pole hidden from view?
Those are Santa Clouds.

What do you call St. Nick's fingernails?
Santa Claws.

How does Santa convince himself to give away so many presents?
He looks in the mirror and says,
"Just be clause."

Why is Santa so jolly?
Because he's Santa.

2
That Christmas Magic
We hope you're enchanted with these jokes
about flying reindeer, magical elves, and other
fantastically festive Christmas creatures!

Which of the reindeer is out of this world?
Comet!

Which reindeer actually prefers
Valentine's Day to Christmas?
Cupid.

Which of the reindeer loves mornings?
Dawner!

What did Mrs. Claus say to Santa when she saw clouds?
"It looks like rain, dear."

What do baby reindeer call their mothers?
Mommy Deer-ist.

Where do reindeer go for coffee?
Starbucks.

How much did Santa pay for his reindeer?
I don't know, but he must have paid deer-ly.

What quacks and guides Santa's sleigh?
Rudolph the Red-Nosed Rein-Duck.

Which of Santa's reindeer has the worst manners?
Rude-dolph.

Which of Santa's reindeer is the fastest?
Dasher!

Why does Rudolph's nose shine even when he isn't awake?
Because he's a light sleeper.

Did you hear
Rudolph needed
braces?
Yep. Buckteeth.

**What's furry, brings presents, and falls
from the sky?**
Rain-deer!

How does Rudolph know when it's Christmas?
He looks at his calen-deer.

Who rules over Dasher and the rest?
A reign-deer.

Why did Rudolph's grades slip?
Because he went down in history.

Santa's reindeer got annoyed when they were left next to a tall building.
But they got over it.

How did Santa's reindeer with no left legs turn out?
All right!

What's the difference between a knight and a reindeer?
A knight slays a dragon, while a reindeer drags a sleigh.

Why do reindeer fly?
They can't seem to get their drivers' licenses.

How do you make a reindeer fast?
Don't feed it much.

What do you call a three-eyed reindeer?
A reiiindeer.

What's the number one reindeer game?
Stable tennis.

Why does Rudolph go so fast?
Because there are eight reindeer and a flying sleigh right behind him!

What happened when Rudolph shined his nose into a cloud?
It made a rein-bow!

Which of
Santa's reindeers
loves to party?
Dancer!

Which reindeer is full of cream cheese?
Blintzen.

How did the team of reindeer win the big North Pole football game?
Blitzen.

Where do Santa's reindeer stop for ice cream when their job is done?
Deery Queen.

What do reindeer eat for breakfast?
Deer-ios.

Which of Santa's reindeer can jump higher than a roof?
They all can—roofs can't jump.

Which reindeer is always fully dressed?
Pantser.

What's brown, white, and red all over?
A sunburned reindeer.

**Did you hear Santa couldn't use reindeer,
so he used wet cows instead?**
They were rain-steer.

Which reindeer always turned in perfectly punctuated homework?
Dasher.

What reindeer delivers food as a side gig?
Door Dasher.

What kind of pictures do Santa's helpers love to take?
Elfies!

What Kind of
cameras do
those elves use?
Polaroids.

Where do elves vote in elections?

At the North Poll.

What's green, white, and red all over?

An elf trying on Santa's suit.

What game do elves like to play?

Gift tag.

Why did the elves make a big batch of suckers?

Because 'tis the season to be lolly!

Why do elves
hear every
secret uttered
at the North Pole?
Because they're
all ears.

Why did everyone in the
workshop have to take baths?
Because they were all elfully smelly.

Why do Santa's helpers eat outside?

They just prefer to dine elf-fresco.

Is Santa's workshop open on Christmas?

No, it's Claused.

A visiting elf knew all the elves at the North Pole.

What a small world!

What's an elf's favorite sport? Miniature golf.

How do the elves congratulate Santa when he returns?
With Sant-applause!

Why is there an Elf on the Shelf?
Because "Elf on the Table" doesn't rhyme.

Why is Santa's workshop at the North Pole?
The rent is too high at the South Pole.

How do the elves get to
the workshop each day?
In minivans.

Did you hear they're doing the Winter Olympics at the workshop?
It's mostly just North Pole vaulting.

The elf argued that his ears were better than Santa's.
He had some good points.

What do you call an elf who just won the lottery?
Welfy.

Who is the best singer in the North Pole?
Elfish Presley.

How do elves cook Christmas dinner?
With u-tinsels.

Santa used to have twelve helpers but one left.
How many does he have now?
Elf-even.

Why couldn't Santa's elf pay rent?
He was a little short.

What do elves learn in elf preschool?
The elf-abet.

Why can't Santa work in a small workshop?
He gets Claustrophobic.

What do you call an elf who walks backward?
A fle!

What do the quietest elves in the workshop make?
Sssh-elves.

Does Santa have a boss?
No, he's elf-employed.

Hey, they're not merely workshop elves.
They're subordinate Clauses.

What do the elves do on December 24?
They wrap things up!

3
The Perfect Gift

Consider this collection of jokes about Christmas presents to be our Christmas present to you.

I just love the look of a Christmas tree with gifts underneath. It has so much presents!

Where's the best place to find whittle gifts?
The gift shop!

Did you hear about the kid who could tell what was inside of a wrapped present just by looking at it?
It's a gift!

What kind of musicians give out the best gifts? Wrappers!

What was left on the floor after all the kids opened their Christmas gifts?

It was a Christ-mess!

Why didn't the rope get any Christmas presents?

It was too knotty.

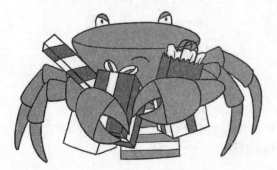

Why don't crabs give out Christmas presents?
They're shellfish.

How do lambs get their presents
for each other?
They go sheeping.

**Why do some jungle cats wind up on Santa's
naughty list?**
Because they're cheetahs!

**What did the chicken like best about
Christmas presents?**
The bocks.

Which athletes leave the
nicest presents under the tree?
Boxers!

**What do you call Christmas gifts already
under the tree?**
Present!

MOM: Don't buy your dad a drill for Christmas.
KID: Why not?
MOM: It's boring.

You write a letter to Santa, and then you get toys.

This is what's known as Claus and effect.

They say that in giving a gift, it's the thought that counts.

That's what's called "presents of mind."

Which dinosaurs are good at putting presents together? Veloci-wrappers.

Who always knows exactly what they're getting for Christmas?
Santa!

Why does Santa deliver presents on Christmas Day?
Because it's a holiday, and the post office is closed.

What do you call a kid who doesn't like Santa? A rebel without a Claus!

Did you hear about the kid who
wrapped 20 gifts in 10 minutes?
She was on a roll!

**Who steals presents from the rich, wraps them,
and gives them to the poor?**
Ribbon Hood.

Want to hear a joke about wrapping paper?
Never mind, it's tearable.

What kind of dogs deliver
beautiful presents under the tree?
Boxers.

I bought my parents a refrigerator for Christmas.
They opened it, and how their faces lit up!

How is Christmas unlike other holidays?
You can box it up!

Why was the unwrapped gift unhappy?
It felt boxed in.

Why are books bad Christmas gifts?
Because the recipient has to take them back to the library!

Why do kids tear all the paper off of their presents? Because they love them to pieces!

BROTHER: I thought about buying you a present.
SISTER: But you didn't!
BROTHER: Hey, it's the thought that counts.

What do a gassy guy and kids on Christmas have in common?

They both let 'er rip.

What kind of dogs get the most Christmas presents?
Golden receivers!

What's the best gift for an archer? It doesn't matter, as long as you include a bow!

Kids at Christmas never worry much about the New Year.
They're too focused on the present.

What's another name for the ghost from *A Christmas Carol*?
Christmas Presence!

I went Christmas shopping with my friend Holly. She didn't buy anything, but then she helped me put up my decorations. I decked the halls with browsing Holly.

The only gifts I have to buy this year are for my feline friends.
So I'm doing all my shopping from a catalog.

What did the wrapping paper say to the Christmas tree?
"Cousin, is that you?"

KID: Hey, Dad, what do you want for Christmas?
DAD: Nothing would make me happier than a brand-new guitar.
KID: Great, I'll get you nothing!

KID: Mom, what do you want for Christmas?
MOM: Something with diamonds.
KID: Great, I'll get you a deck of cards!

Doing your Christmas shopping early is a great way to beat the rush.
Except I did mine twelve months early, and all the stores were still busy.

Why did the Christmas shopper get arrested for shopping early?
He went before the store opened.

Why do we open presents on December 25?
Because it's Christmas!

4
Trees and Traditions

Trim the tree with some hee hee hees, and deck the halls with some ha ha has!

How is a Christmas tree like a dog? It's known for its bark.

How do you take care of a dry Christmas tree?
Use plenty of Tannen-balm.

I'm so glad we got a real Christmas tree this year.
It really spruced up the place!

Want to hear a joke about popcorn garland?
Never mind, it's corny.

What did the popcorn garland say to its maker?
"Stop needling me!"

What did the working bulb say to the broken bulb?
"Lighten up!"

Why did the dumb guy eat the Christmas decorations off the house?
For a light snack.

Why was the mistletoe leaf
shaped like a chicken?
It grew up in a poul-tree.

**What did the third of the Three Wise Men say
after the other two offered up their gifts of gold
and frankincense?**
"Wait, there's myrrh!"

KID: What's a Christmas tree made of?
DAD: Wooden you like to know!

How are Christmas trees like blockbuster movies?
They both have stars.

What's another name for a tree skirt?
A fir coat.

Who guards the biggest Christmas trees?
Tinsel-diers.

How do you make a fir tree?
Cross a pinecone and a polar bear!

Why did the Christmas tree go to the doctor?
It was looking a little green.

What kind of dog do you find on Christmas?
A point-setter.

What's the difference between a Christmas plant and a scorekeeper?
One's a point setter and the other's a poinsettia.

What kind of
Christmas tree
is the coziest?
A fir tree.

What did one Christmas tree say to the other?
"I pine for you!"

What is a Christmas tree's favorite candy?
Orna-mints.

Why don't Christmas trees knit?
Because they keep dropping their needles.

Why shouldn't you let a fisherman near the Christmas tree?
They'll want to take all the ornament hooks.

If athletes get athlete's foot, what do astronauts get?
Missle-toe.

What do you use to decorate a canoe for Christmas?
Oar-naments.

What's a barber's favorite Christmas activity?
Trimming the tree.

Did you hear about the cracker's Christmas party?
It was a banger!

When do all the Christmas trees get cut down?
Sep-timber.

Why did the Three Wise Men bring gifts?
To have a myrrh-y Christmas!

What fruit
grows on
Christmas trees?
Pine-apples.

Why was the cat afraid of the Christmas tree?
The bark!

**What would you find in the duck pond at
the North Pole?**
Duck-orations.

How did Santa destroy a house with one step inside?
It was a gingerbread house.

How do they decorate the ocean for Christmas?
With reefs!

How did the snow globe feel on Christmas Day?
Shaken!

What's the most Christmas-y part of the ocean?
The yuletide.

What Christmas decorations are always leaning over?
The boughs of holly.

Why did the kid punch the wall with tinsel?
He wanted to deck the halls.

Where does mistletoe come from?
On the mistle-tow truck.

What's crumbly and full of prizes and jokes?
A Christmas cracker.

Where does a Christmas tree keep all its stuff?
In its trunk.

The tree used to be a regular tree until it took on some decorations.
Talk about branching out.

No matter the size, what shape is every Christmas tree?
A tree-angle.

Cats take forever to shop and wrap and bake.
They just want everything to be purrrrrfect.

Why are advent calendars sad?
Their days are clearly numbered.

This year, we have a huge Tannenbaum.
It's tree-mendous!

Why do people hang lights on their houses?
Because they'd get crushed in the driveway.

Why does Santa wear a red suit? Because he hates ugly Christmas sweaters.

Which monsters' Christmas trees look the best? Mummies, because they're so good at wrapping.

What do ornaments do when they get together?

They just hang out.

What's the king of Christmas?

The stock-king.

The angel on top of the tree was a perfect square.

It was a right angel.

Where's the best place to buy Christmas decorations?
Hollywood.

Why was the ornament so into Christmas trees?
He got hooked at an early age.

I just saw a bunch of snow-covered Christmas trees at the Christmas tree lot.
I guess what they say is true: Firs in the weather flock together.

Why couldn't the kid hang any ornaments on the white-coated Christmas tree?
She was flocked out.

What happened to the Christmas tree that saw the Halloween decorations in the garage?
It got so scared it turned into petrified wood!

Why did the couple get married on December 25?
They wanted to have a marry Christmas.

What do you call a person who tells Christmas jokes?
A Christmas card!

How does Rudolph decorate his antlers?
With some horn-aments.

Where's the best place to find a Christmas tree?
Between Christmas two and Christmas four!

What do you call a leg pain that ruins Christmas?
A leg Krampus.

What do you call cutting your own tree?
Christmas chopping.

What happens if you get arrested for stealing an advent calendar?
You get a month.

What's the most popular thing kids give their parents at Christmas?
A list!

What's got a big hole in it but contains abundant treasures? A Christmas stocking!

What do pirates send out on Christmas?
Carrrrrrrds.

What should you do if it's midnight on Christmas Eve and you still haven't finished *A Christmas Carol*?
Book it!

What you do call an angry rodent named Mary who lives under a Christmas tree?
Mary Cross-Mouse!

What's a squirrel's favorite Christmas production?
The Nutcracker.

How do you greet the angel on top of the tree?
"Halo!"

What makes a good Christmas star?
If it's out of this world!

What do you call a boring Christmas?
A Feliz Navi-dud.

Where do you find mistletoe?
In a mistle-shoe.

How do you grow the perfect Tannenbaum?
Learn some chemis-tree.

Do they have Christmas in the ocean?
Yep, 'tis the sea-son!

What Christmas decoration is full of medicine?
An IV.

What did the candy cane say to the tree ornament?
Hang in there!

What do Christmas and a beach cat have in common?
Sandy Claws.

Everyone loves Christmas.
Why? Well, as far as holidays go, it's extremely Santa-mental.

What's a bird's favorite Christmas tale?
How the Finch Stole Christmas.

How do werewolves wish each other happy holidays? "Hairy Christmas!"

Did you hear how Scrooge's team won the football game?
The Ghost of Christmas passed!

I dropped my copy of *A Christmas Carol* on my foot.
It hurt like the Dickens.

What kind
of dog does
Scrooge have?
A hum-pug.

What does Scrooge eat on Christmas?
Humbug-ers.

What did the grandma light string say to the kid light string?
"My, how you've glown!"

What does a Christmas-hating sheep say?
"Baaaaaa humbug!"

Is turning off a Christmas decoration display fun to watch?
Sure, it's de-lightful!

I just wrote a whole book on tinsel.
Paper would have been easier.

Why was the Christmas tree uncomfortable?
Pines and needles!

Why should you always let your Aunt Claire decorate your house for Christmas?
So your stockings are hung by the chimney, with Claire.

What are stockings filled with when it isn't Christmas?
Feet!

5
A-Caroling We Will Go
You don't even have to be named Carol to enjoy
these jokes about the music of Christmas!

What Christmas song do they
sing in the desert?
"Oh Camel Ye Faithful."

What can you hurt if you sing Christmas songs too loud?
Your tinsils!

What's hard, covered in decorations, and goes "ting-a-ling-a-ling"?
A jingle bell rock.

What Christmas song would you probably hear at the library?
"Silent Night."

What has 100 feet and sings?
Fifty carolers.

How do Christmas carolers buy their presents?
With har-money.

How do jockeys prepare for Christmas Day races?
With one horse, soap, and hay!

Where would you find the most Christmas song singers?
In North and South Carolina.

Why should you take a ladder when you go Christmas caroling? So you can hit the high notes!

What happens when you
teach ducks to do ballet?
They'll perform The Nutquacker.

Who is Santa's favorite singer?
Beyon-sleigh.

What's another name for Father Christmas?
Feliz Navidad!

Have you heard that song about the Christmas tree that stayed out in the sun?
It's called "O Tan-nenbaum."

Did you know that there's a
Christmas song about Swiss cheese?
"O Holey Night."

**How does Good King Wenceslas like his
pizza styled and cooked?**
Deep and crisp and even.

**Every time I hear a Christmas song, I throw a
pebble into the air and then catch it.**
It's my jingle bell rock!

What's the most anxious Christmas song?

"Do You Hear What I Hear?"

What's the grossest Christmas song?

"All I Want for Christmas is Ewwwww."

There wasn't a cloud in the sky or a flake of snow in the December 25 weather forecast.

Talk about a blue Christmas.

How do you wish your sailor father merry Christmas?
"Feliz Navy-dad!"

I don't like "The 12 Days of Christmas."
It's for the birds!

My friend David's family has this odd tradition going back a dozen generations where the next son is born on December 25th. We call them the Twelve Daves of Christmas.

Why were the ten lords a-leaping?
To get out of the way of the nine ladies dancing.

What's the best song about Santa getting ready for Christmas Eve? "Hair Combs Santa Claus."

What's the name of the horse in "Jingle Bells"?
Bob, because bells on Bob's tails ring.

Why were the seven swans a-swimming?

They didn't want to do anything so noisy that they'd wake up the six geese a-laying.

Why were the twelve drummers drumming?

Because all the maids a-milking and ladies dancing positions had been filled.

What's an avocado's favorite Christmas song? "Guacing in a Winter Wonderland."

What do the three French hens in "The 12 Days of Christmas" lay?
French eggnog.

Did you know that Rudolph the Red-Nosed Reindeer used to be called something else?
Yeah, all of the other reindeer used to laugh and call him Names.

What's the best song about Santa driving his sleigh?
"Do You Steer What I Steer?"

What's a song about how Santa likes to prank kids with some coal in their stocking?
"Santa Claus is Coming to Clown."

What's the most popular Christmas song in Italy?
"There's No Place Like Rome for the Holidays."

When did Santa bring presents to the swamp?
One froggy Christmas Eve.

What's the best song about Christmas shopping?
"Deck the Malls."

KID 1: Did you like the Christmas carol?
KID 2: I sure did.
KID 1: But you didn't sing at all.
KID 2: Yeah, it was "Silent Night."

MOM: Why did you bring in a bunch of ghosts singing carols?
KID: I wanted to get into the holiday spirit!

How do you wish a detective a merry Christmas?
"Police Navidad!"

Dwayne Johnson is so tall he can stretch his arms around the Tannenbaum.
That's a Rock around the Christmas tree!

What kind of Christmas songs
are sung underwater?
Christmas corals!

A bunch of nuts were sitting in the hallway making fun of each other.

They were chestnuts roasting in an open foyer.

We decorated a boulder with lights and tinsel.

Now it's a jingle bell rock.

Why is Santa great at grocery shopping?

Because he makes a list and checks it twice.

What does a barber sing at Christmas?
"O Comb All Ye Faithful"

What's a Christmas carol to be sung in your backyard?
"Deck the Halls."

Where does Santa spend his money?
On his jingle bills.

What kind of bells does Santa put on his sleigh?
Kringle bells!

How do you wish a lamb a happy holiday?
Sing "We Wish Ewe a Merry Christmas."

What's a wolf's favorite Christmas song?
"Deck the Howls."

What's a dog's favorite Christmas song?
"Bark, the Herald Angels Sing."

Why couldn't the pony sing a Christmas song?
Because it was a little hoarse.

I don't know why people think Santa is so hard to catch.
It says right there in that song, he lives on Santa Claus Lane.

How do you sing Christmas carols if you don't know the words?
Just Bethle-hum.

What's festive and stinks?
Jingle smells!

Where can you get the eggs
for Christmas breakfast?
From the three French hens!

What's an elf's favorite Christmas song?
"I'll Be Gnome for Christmas."

How do you wish a sheep a merry Christmas?
"Fleece Navidad!"

What Christmas song makes you cringe?
"Good King Wince-eslas."

What's the best present
for the Little Drummer Boy?
A broken drum—it can't be beat!

What kind of dogs could pull Santa's sleigh?
Wiener dogs, because they don't mind dachshund through the snow!

What happened when lightning hit the tree lot?
There was shocking around the Christmas trees!

How do you wish your friend Carol a happy holiday?
"It's Christmas, carol!"

6
A Plate of Milk and Cookies

*Enjoy these tasty jokes about holiday
treats and Christmas foods.*

How did the
gingerbread man
get around after
he broke his leg?
With a candy cane.

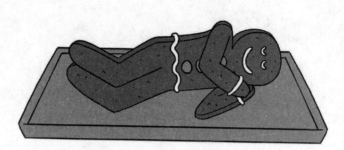

What do gingerbread men sleep on?
Cookie sheets.

Why did Santa eat the whole plate of cookies?
Because he was ho-ho-hungry.

What Christmas treat shouldn't you eat?
Crackers!

Why are cranberries part of Christmas dinner?
'Tis the season to be jelly!

How do you make Christmas sandwiches?
With mistle-toast.

Why did the turkey skip Christmas dinner?

It was already stuffed.

What's red, white, and blue at Christmas?

A sad candy cane.

What's Santa's favorite sandwich?

Peanut butter and jolly.

What does Santa eat with his sandwich?
Crisp Pringles.

Why did the baker give away tons of Christmas cookies?
He had a lot of dough!

Why did the Christmas cookie go to the doctor? It was feeling crumby.

What kind of sausage does Santa prefer?
North Polish sausage.

Why won't snowmen eat carrot cake?
They don't want to eat their own noses!

Never invite the Polar Express to Christmas dinner.
It choo-choos with its mouth open!

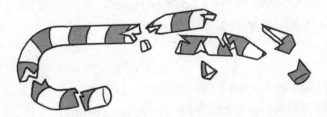

Why did the candy cane get
shattered into little pieces?
Because it was Christmas break.

What's a
snowman's
favorite part of
the Christmas cake?
The icing.

Does celery make a good present?
Sure, but only as a stalking stuffer.

KID: Can I have a bike for Christmas?
**MOM: No, you can have Christmas dinner
like everyone else.**

What smells the best at Christmas dinner?
Your nose!

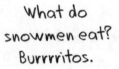

What do
snowmen eat?
Burrrritos.

What's invisible and smells like cookies and milk?
Santa's burps.

Why shouldn't you eat an entire Yule log?
Because yule regret it.

How do elves make sandwiches?
With shortbread!

What do you call it when you spill cookie icing on your Christmas clothes?
A Christmas sweeter.

What do naughty kids eat on Christmas?
Coal-slaw.

What did the gingerbread man do for his leg injury?
Iced it.

What do naughty kids eat for breakfast?
Co-Coal Puffs.

What do Christmas chickens make?

Eggnog.

What are the sneakiest Christmas treats?

Mince spies.

**For Christmas breakfast, we always have eggs
Benedict on metal plates.**

Because there's no place like chrome for the hollandaise.

Why do dogs
want to eat
candy canes?
They just
love peppermint.

What holiday
treat do
pirates treasure?
Chestnuts.

What are the funniest Christmas cookies?
Snickerdoodles!

Those candy canes are so nice.
They must be in mint condition.

I love the smell of cookies and candles and incense.
Christmas just makes a lot of scents.

What side dish do your parents' parents always bring to Christmas dinner?

Gran-berry sauce.

We ate a Christmas feast consisting entirely of cranberries, cherries, and strawberries.

You could say that we had ourselves a berry Christmas.

Why did the kid wake up with a headache on Christmas?

Visions of sugar plums danced in his head.

What food do they serve in the cafeteria at Santa's workshop?

Brrrrr-grrrrs!

What else do they serve?

Chili!

What do snowmen eat for breakfast?
Ice Krispies.

Why is December the best time to buy herbs and spices?
Because it's the most wonderful thyme of the year.

How do you make a wet salad at the North Pole?
Lettuce, snow, lettuce, snow, lettuce, snow!

What do snowmen bring to potlucks?
Cold slaw!

Which vegetables grow best at the North Pole?
Snow peas.

Why do so many people drink eggnog around the holidays?
It's everywhere—you can't egg-nore it!

What has green leaves, red berries,
and smells like fish?
Holly mackerel.

What's full of nuts and smells like farts?
Tootcake.

How do you roast beef for Christmas?
Gently tease it.

KID: Hey, did you buy that cake?
DAD: No, it's stollen!

When is it frosty inside during Christmastime?
When you're frosting cookies!

Which Christmas character is made entirely of sugar?
Frosting the Snowman.

What's red, white, and sharp?
A broken candy cane.

How is baseball like a Christmas cookie? Both depend on the batter.

How is fruitcake like a history textbook?
It's full of dates.

DAD: Did you eat all the Christmas cookies for Santa?
KID: I didn't touch one of them.
DAD: Then why is only one left?
KID: Well, that's the one I didn't touch.

How do basketball players eat their Christmas cookies?
They dunk them.

My grandmother's recipe for Christmas cookies is top secret.
It's on a knead-to-know basis.

Why should you never prank a glass of eggnog?
Because it just can't take a yolk.

I've kept track of every Yule log I've burned and every Yule log I've eaten.

It's all right there in my log-log-blog.

Why did Santa get a tummy-ache?

He ate too many Ho Ho Hos.

7
Winter Wonderland

*Warm up by laughing at these jokes about ice,
snow, and other chilly, wintry stuff.*

What can you
catch in the
winter with
your eyes closed?
A cold!

How do snowmen get 'round?
They ride an icicle.

I made a wonderful snowman and thought it would come to life. It didn't.
Talk about a Frosty reception.

What did one snowman say to the other?
"Do you smell carrots?"

What's white, sparkly, and travels up into the sky?
A confused snowflake.

What do snowmen do on their phones?
They surf the winternet.

What falls on Christmas but doesn't get hurt?
Snow!

Somebody knocked over the snowman I built, but we never found out who.
It's a cold case.

What's a snowman's favorite game?
Freeze tag!

What's the difference between the law and an ice block?

One is justice; the other is just ice.

What happens when a snowman gets upset?

It has a meltdown.

Why is snow white and cold?

Because if it were red and hot it would be lava.

I just heard a snowman saying "C-O-L-D" over and over again. It must be a cold spell.

Why did the snow shoveler love her work?
Because there's no business like snow business!

KID: What do you think snowmen think about?
MOM: Snow idea!

How do you celebrate a well-made snowman?
You sing "Freeze a jolly good fellow"!

What do
you call a snowball
with teeth?
Frostbite!

Why did the kid go to school wearing only one snow boot? Because the forecast called for a 50 percent chance of snow.

I wish I knew what this Christmas village we stumbled on was called.

I guess it's just a winter wonderland.

Why shouldn't you wear snow boots?

They'll melt!

Why shouldn't you tell jokes
while ice skating?
You don't want to crack up the lake!

Why does Jack Frost get invited to all the Christmas parties?
Because he's just so cool.

How do you lift a frozen car?
With a Jack Frost.

What's cold, sweet, and shows up around Christmastime?

Jack Frosting.

KID: Do you like the cold weather?
DAD: To a certain degree.

When is a ship like snow?

When it's adrift!

What do you call an iguana
lost at the North Pole?
A blizzard!

People act like the North Pole and the South Pole are exactly the same.
Actually, they're an entire world apart.

What did the hat say to the scarf?
"You hang out. I'll go on a head."

In speed-sledding contests, there are winners.
And then there are lugers.

What do you call little snowmen?
Chill-dren.

What do you call a snowman that
can do a thousand crunches?
The Abdominal Snowman!

**Did you hear about the outdoor boxing match
at the North Pole?**
Both fighters were out cold.

**What do you call an ice floe that gives you a
Christmas present?**
A niceberg!

What do you call a weird snowman?
Flaky.

What do
North Pole
elves wear
on their heads?
Snowcaps!

How do snowmen spend their weekends?

They pretty much just chill.

How do you make yellow snow?

Make a snowman laugh really *hard!*

What makes you warm at Christmas but is too hot itself?

A Christmas sweater!

What do you
call a snowman
on roller skates?
A snowmobile.

What do you call a lady snowman?
A snow ma'am.

Why is snow so comforting at Christmas?
Because there's snow place like home.

Why did the snowman buy a bag of carrots?
He wanted to pick his nose!

What exercises do gymnasts do in the winter?
Winter-saults!

Which season is the best?

Winter. Because it's way cooler than all the others!

What's the coldest month of the year?

Decem-brrrr!

Why do polar bears hibernate all winter?

Well, nobody is going to go wake up a bunch of polar bears.

Why did the polar bear flunk out of school?
Its grades were all at least twenty below zero!

What kind of socks does a Christmas bear wear?
None—they go around with bear feet!

What's Jack Frost's favorite school activity?
Snow-and-tell.

What's cold, white, and jingles?
Snowbells!

What's the hardest thing about learning to skate?
The ice!

8 .
Special Delivery
*Knock-knock jokes, riddles, tongue twisters,
and more Christmas surprises.*

Knock-knock!
Who's there?
Cole.
Cole who?
Cole is not
what I want
in my stocking
this year.

Knock-knock!
Who's there?
Dishes.
Dishes who?
Dishes a nice
place to put a
Christmas wreath!

Knock-knock!
Who's there?
Needle.
Needle who?
Needle little help decorating the tree?

Knock-knock!
Who's there?
Ribbon.
Ribbon who?
Ribbon open presents is a blast!

Knock-knock!
Who's there?
Avery.
Avery who?
Avery merry Christmas to you!

Knock-knock!
Who's there?
Doughnut.
Doughnut who?
Doughnut open your gifts until Christmas!

Knock-knock!
Who's there?
Dewey.
Dewey who?
Dewey know how long it is until Santa gets here?

Knock-knock!
Who's there?
Gladys.
Gladys who?
Gladys finally Christmas—how about you?

Knock-knock!
Who's there?
Ginger.
Ginger who?
Gingerbread man!

Knock-knock!
Who's there?
Honda.
Honda who?
Honda first day of Christmas my true love sent to me . . .

Knock-knock!
Who's there?
Howard.
Howard who?
Howard you like to go Christmas caroling?

Knock-knock!
Who's there?
Hannah.
Hanna who?
Hanna partridge in a pear tree!

Knock-knock!
Who's there?
Holly.
Holly who?
Holly-days are here again!

Knock-knock!
Who's there?
Ima.
Ima who?
Ima excited for Christmas!

Knock-knock!
Who's there?
Justin.
Justin who?
Justin time for Christmas!

Knock-Knock!
Who's there?
Holly.
Holly who?
Holly up and
let me in.
It's cold out here!

Knock-knock!
Who's there?
Kanye.
Kanye who?
Kanye help me pick out a Christmas tree?

Knock-knock!
Who's there?
Lettuce.
Lettuce who?
Lettuce in for hot cocoa and Christmas cookies, please.

Knock-knock!
Who's there?
Pikachu.
Pikachu who?
Pikachu Christmas presents and you'll be in trouble!

Knock-knock!
Who's there?
Santa.
Santa who?
Santa letter to the North Pole—hope it arrives in time.

Knock-knock!
Who's there?
Yule.
Yule who?
Yule know when you answer the door.

Knock-knock!
Who's there?
Reindeer.
Reindeer who?
Reindeer last night instead of snowed.

Knock-knock!
Who's there?
Abby.
Abby who?
Abby New Year!

Knock-knock!
Who's there?
Christmas.
Christmas who?
Christmas be my lucky day!

Knock-knock!
Who's there?
Yule log.
Yule log who?
Yule log the door after you let me in, won't you?

Knock-knock!
Who's there?
Rufus.
Rufus who?
Rufus covered in snow!

Knock-knock!
Who's there?
Centipede.
Centipede who?
Centipede after he drank all that milk to wash down
the cookies.

Knock-knock!
Who's there?
Peas.
Peas who?
Peas tell me what you got me for Christmas!

Knock-knock!
Who's there?
Norway.
Norway who?
Norway I'm kissing under the mistletoe.

Knock-knock!
Who's there?
The Grinch.
The Grinch who?
No, the Grinch hates the Whos!

Knock-knock!
Who's there?
Noah.
Noah who?
Noah good place to go Christmas shopping?

Knock-knock!
Who's there?
Macon.
Macon who?
Macon a list and checking it twice!

Knock-knock!
Who's there?
Santa!
At the door? Why not the chimney, Santa?

"Are we not having goose for Christmas dinner?"
Tom asked, in a fowl mood.

"Now I have the tools to head to the Christmas tree farm,"
said Tom, with a heavy accent.

"Here's all the money you'll need to buy presents for
everyone," Tom advanced.

"I'm halfway up the mountain!" the Grinch alleged.

"I love making Christmas cookies
into festive shapes," Tom cut in.

"I don't have any hair!" the snowman bawled.

"Let's not sing 'Silent Night'!" Tom allowed.

"I've mailed my letter to Santa," Tom assented.

"Keep that fire lit and Santa won't be able to arrive!" Tom bellowed.

"I wonder how many reindeer Santa originally had," Tom said considerately.

"I manufacture tabletops for Santa's workshop," Tom counterproductively said.

"I just came in through the chimney," said Santa, entranced.

"I see," said Jack Frost.

"I cut down trees at a Christmas tree farm," Tom lumberingly said.

"What's the value of a letter to Santa?" Tom noteworthily asked.

"Is it Christmas yet?" Tom asked periodically.

"I have a gift for you," Tom said presently.

"I can't believe I ate so many cookies,"
Santa said heavily.

"I couldn't believe the elves made exactly four billion toys!"
Santa recounted.

"I just bought a wool Christmas sweater,"
said Tom sheepishly.

"Let's sing 'Holly Jolly Christmas,'" Tom said soberly.

Santa went down, lickety-split,
Forgetting to see if a fire was lit.
He flew out of the chimney
While dancing a shimmy.
His job is quite hard, he'll admit.

There once was a little elf named Fred
Who lived in a house of gingerbread.
Though tasty, those walls
Dissolved in snowfalls
And left crumbs all over Fred's bed.

An elf said to Santa, "Oh, dear!
We didn't make enough presents, alas!"
That made Santa think
How that really did stink,
So instead, he just gave the kids cash.

Kris Kringle carefully crunches candy canes.

Eggnog, Yule log.

It's sweater weather whether you wear the sweater or not.

Santa stacked six swaying snowmen in his sleigh.

Harry hung holly on the hearth for the holidays.

Red bulb, blue bulb.

Chrissy wishes for Christmas kisses.

Claus's cat claws in the closet.

Cooks cook Christmas cookies quickly.

Saint Nick clicked six thick bricks.

Pointed poinsettias pop precious presents.

Tiny Tim trimmed the tall tree with tinsel.

Prancer presents pumpkin pies and presents.

Pretty packages perfectly packed in paper.

Santa's sack sags slightly in the snowy sleigh.

Comet cuddles cute Christmas kittens carefully.

What goes "ho, ho, ho, plop?"
Santa, laughing his head off.

Why is Christmas the champion of holidays, always getting the W?
Because it has noel.

Can you describe a snow-covered road with just two letters?
I *and* C.

What always comes at the end of Christmas?
The letter S.

What's in December that you won't find in any other month?
The letter D.

What flies, has a shell, comes in pairs,
and makes a great Christmas gift?
A turtle dove!

What ball doesn't bounce?
A snowball.

When does Christmas come before Thanksgiving?
In the dictionary!

What kind
of bug hates
Christmas?
A humbug.

What do you get when you cross an archer with a gift-wrapper?
Ribbon Hood.

What kind of bank doesn't contain any money?
A snowbank.

You throw this during the holidays but never catch it. What is it?

A Christmas party!

What's festive and has an upstairs?

A Christmas story.

How many presents can Santa fit in his empty sack?

One—after that, it isn't empty anymore.

What flies at birth, lies when alive, and runs when it dies?

Snow.

What time does Christmas Day start?

As early as possible!

What time of day is 12:25?
Christmastime!

What's round, the size of a dot, and festive?
The Christmas period.

In what year does New Year's Eve come before Christmas?
Every year!